FRACTURED FAMILIES

Fractured Families

The untold anguish
of the falsely accused

BFMS

This edition published by BFMS, 2007

British Library Cataloguing in Publication Data
Data available

ISBN 978 0 9555184 0 9

British False Memory Society
Bradford on Avon
Wiltshire
BA15 1NF
www.bfms.org.uk

Registered Charity No. 1040683

Printed and bound in the UK by Lightning Source.

*To Roger Scotford who worked tirelessly
to provide a foundation for the voice
of those falsely accused due to false memories.*

Contents

All names and places mentioned in the families' accounts have been changed to protect privacy with the exception of Maxine's story which is already in the public domain. Where pseudonyms are used any similarity to the name of a real person is coincidental and unintended.

ACKNOWLEDGEMENTS

We owe enormous thanks to Norman Brand who first came to us with the idea of putting together a collection of family stories to present to policy makers. Norman, a retired Press Association parliamentary journalist, was the ideal person to listen to the heart-rending, often long and involved accounts which he then skilfully edited.

We are indebted to the families who have bravely told their stories so that others might learn from their harrowing experiences. We thank also the many families who dearly wanted their stories to be told – we could have filled three volumes.

Thank you to Anne Atkins and Professor Larry Weiskrantz who provided valuable contributions to this book. Thank you also to Richard Webster whose advice helped us to make the technical leap from 'pamphlet' to 'book'.

Foreword by Anne Atkins

Some years ago, I went to Zambia and Namibia for a month to research my next novel. I took copious notes in the form of a hardback exercise book, the precious fruit of my travels. When I wanted to start writing a few weeks later, however, I discovered to my devastation that I couldn't find my journal. It wasn't in my suitcase, my bookshelves, my study. I was beside myself. I searched everywhere, asked the housekeeper of a recent host to ransack his drawers, begged my friends and family to rack their brains.

As it happens I was also rather tired and overworked at the time (the natural result of having four young children and a limited family income) so my GP suggested a reputable hypnotist. She thought it might reduce my stress levels: I thought of my diary. Perhaps the hypnotist could delve deep into my buried memories and discover where I had mislaid it?

She lived in respectable suburbia, and was clearly a principled and responsible practitioner. (She was also kind: when she realised my financial worries, she charged me a fraction of her usual fee.) She told me of the wonderful benefits of her trade: when she suffered a skiing injury a few winters back, she had stopped the internal bleeding by means of self-hypnotism. I told her of my missing journal; she promised to help. She asked me to lie down, and went through relaxation exercises I was familiar with from drama school. In my mind I lay on an idyllic beach, wandered through beautiful gardens, and imagined a perfect paradise. Soon she was asking me to remember certain things. Some I could, some I couldn't. So when she drew that session to a close, I explained my dilemma: I couldn't always tell what was genuine memory, what imagination. 'That's all right', she said. 'Don't stop and analyse, or make any distinction; simply go along uncritically with anything that comes into your mind. After all the subconscious mind can't lie.'

It was probably at the next session that she helped me track my priceless diary. Again we went through the relaxation routine. Again, she prompted me to remember things. Obedient to her instructions, I suspended my critical faculties and followed any thought that entered my head. I envisaged writing in the book, reading it, and what I had done with it since. With her assistance, I eventually saw a clear picture in my mind of myself putting my diary in my bedside cabinet. There it was, safe and sound, ready for me to find it again. It was strange, because I thought I must have looked in there already, but the memory of that vision was now crystal clear.

I suppose I could be called a moderately sceptical person. I had given hypnotism a go once before, in the hope of finding a harmless way of controlling the excruciating agony of childbirth. The hypnotist told me the pain was all in the mind. He then put a cold metal fork in my hand, and took me through a number of mental exercises to convince me it was hot. At the end of ten minutes or so of this, he asked me whether it was now warm, quite forcefully eliciting and expecting the answer 'yes'. I thought about it. No, I said truthfully; it's just as cold as it was before. He ended the session there and then, in disgust, and told me I was 'not susceptible'. Years later my children laughed at me, and said of course I wasn't: I never do anything just because I've been told to, and am almost completely immune to peer pressure.

But I'm also game to try most things. And this hypnotist was different; she told me exactly what to do. She didn't ask me to lie or pretend; she simply wanted me to trust my thoughts and allow mental images to flourish. I left that session walking on air. I could see my diary in my bedside cabinet, and had watched myself put it there. If you'd asked me to swear on oath in a court of law that I had genuinely done it, I wouldn't have been sure. But it didn't matter, because I would be home in twenty minutes and could check.

The cabinet was empty.

It was the most vivid and convincing proof, if I ever needed it, that False Memory exists. My therapist was benign and responsible. I was robust and fairly cynical. I only saw her for a few sessions, and the issue was an innocuous one. Nevertheless, I was more than half convinced, under her guidance, that what I imagined had happened. But the crucial difference was that I could go home and see.

Suppose, though, I had been visiting her every week for a year or two? Suppose I was already in a vulnerable state? Suppose she had an agenda and was determined to persuade me of something? Suppose someone's reputation or an important relationship hung in the balance? Most important of all, suppose there had been absolutely no objective way of verifying or refuting what I had thought up? It doesn't bear thinking of...

I don't know why this should be, but almost all counselling or therapy I have ever encountered has been profoundly anti-parent. Years ago, Shaun and I went for a day of what is rather gushily referred to as 'marriage enrichment'. I like such delving into what makes you tick and why you fell head over heels for each other all those years ago when he climbed a twelve foot college wall to pick a lone wild rose fluttering in the breeze.

But in one of the sessions, we were supposed to write down, among other things, 'What you most longed for from your parents'. I must have known that the correct answer should have been affection, or time, or my father to read me a bedtime story. But the truth was that I had enjoyed all those things, and lacked for nothing substantial as a child. So I thought hard and wrote the most truthful answer I could: a pony. (Oh, how I longed for my parents to give me a pony! I'm probably still battling hang-ups about it now...). This was definitely the wrong answer. I was sent away and told to answer the question again. It is axiomatic, in enriching our relationships, that we must criticise our parents.

Some years later our daughter suffered a devastating mental illness (Obsessive Compulsive Disorder). Friends persuaded us to go for marriage counselling to help us cope with the stress. At the first session we were asked to describe our parents. I couldn't fault mine: they were (and still are) the kindest, most unselfish and loving people I've ever come across. The counsellor digested this. Then he turned to my husband. 'I'd like to hear Shaun's response,' he said. Presumably for most couples the simple challenge of adjusting to any other family's way of doing things is enough to drive a little wedge between the two of you, when invited to criticise the in-laws. But Shaun confounded him by agreeing. 'They are very wonderful people,' he confirmed.

The therapist didn't give up. 'Have you ever thought,' he said to me, 'how difficult it must be to go through life with perfect parents?'

I was constantly astonished by how those two counsellors, kind, generous people giving their services for free, could turn good into bad. We were proud that our children were such good friends to one another: that, we were told, was because they were so worried about our unstable relationship that they didn't dare step outside the family. We thought we were happy together: that couldn't be so or we wouldn't have gone for help. I longed for another child: our marriage was not in a fit state to have one.

Oddly, we had found the first two or three months very helpful: they occasionally set us positive tasks like cooking a meal for each other, and we were spending several hours a week committed to something together. But as time went by, I found their negative view of our family made me more and more depressed. After nine months I was so distressed by these weekly sessions, on top of our daughter's illness, that I frequently spent four or five days of the week in tears, only recovering just before the next visit. And yet I was also addicted to seeing these two who now knew so much about us. Every chance comment they made had huge impact on me, and I reiterated the sessions endlessly in my mind.

It wasn't until we stopped for the summer that I began to break free. I was happy for the first time in months. I read a book raising hard-hitting scientific objections to psychotherapy. When they rang in September to arrange for us to resume, Shaun said goodbye to counselling. For months I went on arguing with them in my head or my diary, refuting their devastating criticisms.

But this was nothing to what psychotherapy did to our daughter during her illness. All research I've seen indicates that she became ill because of genetic factors. All successful treatment I've heard of has been based on Cognitive Behavioural Therapy. And yet for months she was subjected to the horror of trying to find a cause for her illness in something we had done. The first time she came home from psychotherapy, she told me of some mistake I had made in her childhood. I apologised. The next week it was something else. I apologised again. This went on for months, while her illness continued to rage and flourish, exacerbated by this nonsense. By the time she had been hospitalised, drugged and subjected to such tripe every day for weeks, she could no longer bear to see me. That Christmas she announced she didn't want to come home...

Ironically, what first made her angry with this brainwashing was a comment our counsellors made to us - that she would never get well until we sorted out what they saw as our problems. 'Is that all they think it is,' she stormed, of the ailment that was wrecking her life, 'that they think such a trivial thing could make me well?'

That was five years ago. She is now almost completely better, studying at university, and the most loving and loyal daughter anyone could ever long for. She is bright, and beautiful, and all her kindness and caring for others - and clear-sightedness - returned with her lost health. We had the fifth child our counsellors so disapproved of my wanting, and she proved the biggest factor in her sister's recovery.

We have been very fortunate indeed.

Though, having said that, I never did find my journal. In the end I managed to recall the only definite memory I had, which was of writing it on the plane coming over the Sahara desert. I concluded I must have put it in the pocket of the seat in front of me, and left it there. So I never did write my Africa novel...

Anne Atkins

Anne Atkins is a writer, journalist and author of three novels, *The Lost Child*, *On Our Own* and *A Fine and Private Place*. She is widely recognised as one of Britain's most trenchant commentators on moral and ethical issues, a familiar name on Radio 4's *Today* programme, on television debates, media discussions, and local panels throughout the country.

Introduction

"I can only say with all my heart, how deeply sorry I am for all the terrible pain and anguish that has occurred in the family as a result of my 'memories' regarding your behaviour to me in my childhood, and I do now feel able to retract all 'allegations' linked to such 'memories'."

The greatest wish of many parents lies in this statement. It forms part of a seven page letter of retraction sent by a daughter to her father in an attempt to apologise for falsely accusing him of sexual abuse in her childhood. She explained how she had found herself at a low and vulnerable point in her life when she was drawn into a search for 'the self' and described a period of 'delving into the sub-conscious' in her search to recover repressed memories which resulted in her 'false memories'. False memories for sexual, physical and emotional abuse can be created not only in the therapy consulting room but also as a result of reading self-help literature, joining cults or survivors' groups, watching television or by other authoritative influences.

Claims of 'recovered memories' began to surface in the UK in the late 1980s when there was an upsurge in allegations of abuse that had not always been remembered by the claimants. The driving force behind these claims being the readiness of mental health and child abuse professions to endorse beliefs that childhood sexual abuse, of which the complainant was previously unaware, was in fact the cause of their adult problems. By the time the British False Memory Society (BFMS) began to take shape in 1993, starting life as a group known as Adult Children Accusing Parents, many parents were already bewildered by 'out of the blue' allegations of historical child sexual abuse and at a loss to know where to turn. Magazine and newspaper articles appeared and were followed by radio and television programmes which exposed what was happening. Soon families were getting in touch with the BFMS in their hundreds. The phenomenon was already affecting thousands of families in the USA. Both countries shared the unwelcome influence of self-help literature such as *The Courage to Heal* (Bass and Davis, 1988 - 2002). By the mid-1990s the Royal College of Psychiatrists, the British Psychological Society and the United Kingdom Council for Psychotherapy all produced guidelines to warn their practitioners of the dangers of using regression therapy techniques to help patients and clients recover memories of events they did not remember and which may never have occurred.[1,2,3,4]

In 1994 the American Medical Association (AMA) issued the following statement: 'The AMA considers recovered memories of childhood sexual abuse to be of uncertain authenticity, which should be subject to external verification.'[5] The popular hypothesis is that because of the particular trauma associated with abuse, the victim is unable to retain conscious recall and this could not be explained by just ordinary forgetting and remembering. That such a process exists has not been validated by scientific evidence. But belief in the concept of repression, now frequently absorbed under the label of dissociation for trauma, is still prevalent.

After 13 years of working with the BFMS the most moving and powerful aspect of the work has been to experience the level of anguish and suffering endured by families who, in so many ways, are just like yours and mine. Most parents have attempted to bring their children up to the best of their abilities and to willingly make sacrifices for them, in the way that we all do, because they are our children and we will do almost anything for them. Barring the untimely death of a child there can be little that equates with the pain of losing a child as a result of being falsely accused of the heinous crime of child sexual abuse. The level of indignation we feel at being falsely accused of even a petty matter strikes at our moral being. How can anyone who has not experienced being falsely accused of child sexual abuse ever understand the enormity of such an injustice? We cannot, but we can listen and learn from those who have been caught in the fallout. There is no better way to highlight the seriousness of this problem than to bring together a collection of these stories from families who reveal numerous common features in their heart-rending accounts.

Fortunately, in today's society, much is being done to prevent abuse and to punish with the full force of the law where a crime has been committed. The current cultural climate is rightly one of zero tolerance but such a stance must not be blind to the need to retain common sense and to promote an equitable and thorough investigation into historic allegations of abuse to determine true from false accusations.

Allegations are thrown and yet, in many of these cases, no legal investigation is instigated, leaving an accused person without any opportunity to put their side of the story. This is not a one-sided matter to be left smouldering without attention. Many families are trapped in the grief for the loss of their loved ones and their life as it was before being accused. They have never been allowed to respond to the 'bombshell' that was dropped without warning. It is time to recognise that a plea of innocence, or, as it is more frequently referred to, 'a denial of guilt', does not always equate to being 'in denial'. This caveat has fostered an environment where an individual who is falsely accused is damned if they do and damned if they don't.

This book needs to turn such apathy on its head. It is of vital importance that the spectrum of professions engaged in child protection work and the criminal justice system, including social workers, mental health practitioners, doctors, the police, and lawyers acknowledge the incidence of false allegations and are briefed in the antecedence to false claims. Progress is being made but if it falters there remains a chance that anyone of us could one day, through no fault of our own, unwittingly be drawn into this nightmare world.

Madeline Greenhalgh
Director, BFMS

References

[1] *The Courage to Heal*, Bass, E., Davis, L., Vermilion, first edition in UK 1990 (reprinted on numerous occasions up to 2002).

[2] 'Reported recovered memories of child sexual abuse. Recommendations for good practice and implications for training, continuing professional development and research.' *Psychiatric Bulletin* (1997). Vol 21. 663-665.

[3] 'Guidelines for psychologists working with clients in contexts in which issues related to recovered memories may arise.' *The Psychologist*, Vol 13. 5., May 2000.

[4] 'Notes for Practitioners - Recovered Memories of Abuse,' UKCP, 1996. Published as guidelines by Murdin, L, in *The Psychotherapist*, UKCP, Spring 1997.

[5] *Memories of Childhood Sexual Abuse*, American Medical Association, Council of Scientific Affairs, 1994.

"The notion that the mind protects itself by repressing or dissociating memories of trauma, rendering them inaccessible to awareness is a piece of psychiatric folklore devoid of convincing empirical support"

R J McNally
'Remembering Trauma'
2005

ELISE

A mother's letter to her daughter, offering love, support and the hope that one day they will be reunited again.

Dear Elise, my beautiful child. How troublesome have been these last three years, since that horrible day in March 2003 when you told me that as a child you were raped by your father, his cousin, your grandfathers and your grandmother and that you were beaten by my sister and mother. Finally your husband accused me of having been the coordinator of this 'mess'. Since then I have been living in unreality.

In the beginning I could not believe what I heard and was worried that something wrong was going on in your therapy and that you could commit suicide.

You were always a sweet and a shy young girl. You suffered from the bad relationship between your father and me and from our divorce. But you could always count on the love and support of all the family. You are our only child and everyone treated you as our little princess.

You also suffered when you and I left our home in France and went to live in Brussels where I got a new job. This brought separation from part of the family, your friends and your certainties, to begin a new life. You went through these difficulties and made new friends. A new school and new experiences allowed you to be more open-minded, to be able to take advantage of the new and the old and, happily, to share your holidays with your former friends.

You travelled a lot in your young life because as soon as you finished school you decided to go to university. Again there were more changes, new friends, a new style of lessons and the beginning of a depression. I came to know, some years after, that during that period you also drank, ate and smoked too much.

I moved office to be closer to you 'just in case' and, indeed, it was the case. You came to live with me for some time just to get back on your feet again, thanks to a psychologist friend of mine, and to decide, after a visit to a friend of yours living in London, that your life was there. Well done: you got your First in Chemistry at university, a boyfriend and a job at Cambridge.

You paid the price, however, with a breakdown in 1997 and a one month stay in a specialised hospital for teenage mental disorders. And since then you haven't ceased being in therapy, with some difficult periods when you had to face new situations like moving to Cambridge or changing your job.

My dear child, we have always been very close and you opened your heart very often. When your mind began to wander I was really worried. You were talking of 'facts' I couldn't verify and you had never shown any troubles that sexual violence usually causes.

I could not believe that you were so desperate at that moment and that your therapist or your GP and your husband did nothing for you. My husband and I drove across Europe to see what was really happening and found a shut door.

We met some hours later in the street. You walked away as if I was contagious and your husband tried to threaten mine. What the hell was going on? I contacted your GP because it was important for the therapists to know of such events in order to help you. The answer was that you are adult and you certainly know what to do. There could only be an intervention if you killed someone or were judged to be at risk of suicide.

24

I contacted your previous therapist in London and had the same answer: first of all the client privacy. You see my dear, to protect your privacy they also protect your illness. But not you. I contacted a lawyer in Cambridge but even legally there was nothing to do. You are married and in England the family does not count any more once there is a husband. I was desperate. I felt like they had killed my only child.

I went back home with my sorrow, my questions, my impotence and it took me months to digest and to stop being a victim.

On the internet under 'memories' I found the False Memory Syndrome Foundation in America which directed me to the BFMS and with horror and relief I realised that my story matched with those of hundreds of British families.

Like the other women accusers you are around 30 years old and you are well educated. You have problems with depression. You began to have some 'memories', small pieces of putative recall that you put together day by day finally to 'discover what has really happened'. You talked of 'forgotten memories' which can one day come to light. Even Freud abandoned his theory, how is it possible that such garbage still circulates?

Now I am sure that you have been manipulated because of your fragility, either through a book or your therapists. Someone let you believe there was a monster in your wardrobe: us! How could they be so irresponsible? They are supposed to help people to relieve their sorrow, to find a smile in their lives. How can they let you build your life on such a huge lie?

I am angry with them, I am angry with you. You are cultivated and open-minded. You received love and attention. You are a scientist and you can believe these superstitious 'theories' - such nonsense. I am angry because you hurt me and never talked to me again. You even went to the police claiming that I was harassing you.

At the same time I am empathic with you, my dear girl, because I understand that you are also hurt and you are suffering and you are trying to find a place on earth in which to live peacefully. My greatest hope is that you will one day be strong enough to find this place and come to me again, talk to me, smiling and hugging, like we did before this storm.

SHEILA

Following two years in therapy and having read 'The Courage to Heal', Sheila confronts her parents with allegations that she was abused as a child.

In 1991, when Sheila was 34 years old, she came to see me one afternoon and dropped the bombshell that she had been sexually abused as a child. She said she didn't know who had done it but she said she had been in therapy for two and a half years. My husband and I spent that entire weekend trying to work out who could possibly have done this, putting all the male members of our circle of family, friends and neighbours under suspicion. Sheila told me to get the book *The Courage to Heal* from her sister, Eileen, whom she had told about the abuse about a month before.

Shortly after that I was invited to Sheila's house without her dad, where she told me that her dad had been the abuser, the pictures in her mind becoming clearer every day. During her therapy she had been asked to write a journal (which I was allowed to read). In the journal she talked about the alleged abuse having started 'before she could speak', then later when she was 'three and four years old' and later still when she was 'seven and eight'.

Her father was not allowed to read this under any circumstances and to this day we do not know the exact detail of the accusations. Although there was nothing specific in the journal it contained veiled unspeakable things. She wrote it was 'more of a feeling' of things having happened to her.

This made my husband and me go back through our lives, practically re-living it. Sheila was a very troubled teenager, rebelling at school, therefore not gaining enough qualifications for university.

Eventually she passed more examinations at college and went to university. She went with no idea of what career path she wanted to follow and after two years she left.

She then married and went back into education and became a social worker. The marriage lasted 10 years. It was after the divorce that she went into therapy. We were in close touch at this time but we knew nothing about the therapy until the accusations.

Although we knew nothing of the therapy we were aware of how unwell she looked. Once the accusations were made our third daughter, Marion, decided to support her sister, despite having said right at the beginning: 'Not my dad. Never in a million years'. Things were strained with Eileen for some years, but we are now closer than we have ever been with her, her husband and the children.

Sheila now has a partner and two children whom we have never seen. Marion also has a partner whom we have never met.

It is now 14 years since we spoke with them. All letters, birthday and Christmas cards are returned un-opened.

JENNY

After taking an overdose, teenager Jenny enters a child and adolescent psychiatric unit. Following a protracted series of therapy sessions, Jenny makes accusations of abuse against her father, only for the charges to be thrown out of court.

As I write I have before me a loving card sent to me by my eldest daughter, Jenny, about three months after my marriage broke up. She was then 14 years old. I had reluctantly decided, as most husbands do, that I should be the one to leave the family home and explained to my four children that it was right for them to stay with their mum. But the upheaval distressed all of them, none more than Jenny. As the eldest she felt substantive responsibility to support her troubled mother.

Both before and after sending this card, 'to Dad ... *I love you heaps*', Jenny became increasingly distressed at her parents' separation. Her difficulties were exacerbated by a number of 'usual' teenage problems (boyfriends, schoolwork, self esteem issues etc) and she was encouraged into a counselling relationship with a Community Psychiatric Nurse (CPN), only for her condition to worsen, drastically. She took an overdose.

Within a day or so of discharge from the hospital after this episode she phoned me and asked me to go for a long walk to talk things through. During two hours of conversation it became very clear that she needed to be helped in a supportive environment away from her still struggling mum as she was a significant suicide risk. Being in the medical profession I, with the agreement of her mum, sought the opinion of a local well-respected child psychiatrist.

I didn't realise at the time but this was, by a huge margin, the worst mistake that I have ever made. It led her, by way of a spurious threat to section her under mental health legislation, to a child and adolescent psychiatric unit. However, at the time I felt a sense of overwhelming relief that she was in the hands of professionals.

In this unit, and over many months, she was given no option other than to become estranged from her family (part of the 'therapy' I was subsequently informed). Additionally, she had enforced loss of contact with all her friends. She received no educational input, was inappropriately subjected to a variety of psychotropic drugs, even though she had no mental illness, and exposed to repeated and protracted biased group therapy ('Tell me what you want and I'll believe you' - CPN).

Jenny also underwent a whole series of frightening experiences e.g. being forcibly injected (whilst being held down) with drugs. She also became increasingly distressed, as did my whole family, by my development of a new relationship.

After more than six months of rapid weight loss, commencement of self-harming with blades of various sorts, as well as self inflicted burns from (staff provided) cigarettes, Jenny phoned me late one Friday afternoon. She told me: 'This place is doing my head in' and asked me to discharge her from the child and adolescent psychiatric unit to my new home. She was profoundly disappointed when I insisted that I would need to have the agreement of her consultant first. In the event the consultant advised against it, although she stated that she could not prevent it.

Therefore, with a tremendously heavy heart, I had to ring Jenny and decline her request. She was absolutely devastated. I heard nothing more from her. I had opted to continue to leave her care in the hands of people that I assumed to be capable professionals who were acting in her best interests.

I subsequently became aware that whilst in 'therapy', with the same CPN both outside and inside the unit, Jenny had been encouraged to make anti-parental judgments. The unit in particular encouraged these to be anti-paternal. Then, within a very few weeks of my further 'rejection' of her, as she must have seen it, she accused me (through her specialist nurse as well as her CPN) of both emotional and physical cruelty and then, finally, of actually having repeatedly sexually abused her over many years.

Absolute belief was attached to anything that Jenny alleged or was encouraged to fabricate. The most ill-judged and biased child protection process then saw me charged for various crimes against my own daughter. Her three siblings were outraged by this but my ex-wife, under threat from social services, supported Jenny and went along, without enthusiasm, with a protracted criminal case against me.

After nine months this was finally dismissed out of Crown Court at the plea and directions hearing stage, due to the fact that the judge recognised 'there is not one scintilla of evidence against this man'. Indeed he went on to affirm 'his reputation has been dragged through the mud. He leaves this court without a stain on his character.'

This judgment was made without the judge/court knowing anything of my overwhelmingly strong defence. However, and most regrettably, the child protection professionals disagreed and therefore so much more damage was done to my family. Absurdity continued. During the whole process all four of my children contemplated suicide, two made repeated attempts (one ending up in an intensive care unit) and a third made plans so to do.

The outcome? Other than the near fatalities of two of my children; four very traumatised and damaged children, educational under-achievement, family disintegration and extreme enduring financial hardship. My own 23 year long medical career was seemingly ended and I suffered profound depression. My own suicide became a real option, which would have 'confirmed' my assumed guilt. With regard to my family's wholly mismanaged case; local health and social services spent/wasted in excess of £250,000 creating absolute awfulness. I have personally lost more than £600,000, although this is manifestly insig-nificant compared to the harm sustained by my children. All mediated by professionals.

The legacy? Jenny has emigrated, at the age of 21, to Australia. A reconciliation with my eldest daughter, so long hoped for by all of the rest of my family, now seems improbable. A void is left in my life and I suspect an even larger one in hers. My second daughter, who re-mained loyal and supportive of me, despite being encouraged by the same CPN to make false allegations against me, is now at university. Thankfully my two youngest children now live with me and are both showing signs of recovery emotionally, socially and educationally. I am slowly rebuilding my medical career, unfortunately some way from my previous medical practice. I have also established a professional educa-tional trust aiming to educate professionals about the great care that has to be taken when assessing contested abuse allegations. The ado-lescent unit and its health professionals are now, after a comprehen-sive and damning multi-authored complaint from my own family, as well as five other similarly affected families, under investigation by the local health trust for malpractice. Social Services have provided a sub-stantive apology to me.

SUSANNE

Admitted to a clinic because of anorexia, Susanne later gives police a 28-page statement alleging that her father has abused her. However, much of the statement appears to have been copied from the infamous self-help book, 'The Courage to Heal'.

Our daughter Susanne was very competitive as a child. She would not rest until she had achieved whatever she set her mind on at the time, in contrast to her more laid back younger sister. In 1982 she became ill with depression and anorexia. As she was in her early teens, she missed a lot of school and left with only one GCE O Level. This was not what was expected of her. However, in time she caught up with both her GCE O and A Levels, and in September 1990 attended university for four years, gaining a 2:1 BEd. Honours Degree. The anorexia which had not entirely gone away returned with a vengeance and in 1994 she was admitted to a hospital in Cambridge for six months. After being discharged her weight soon dropped to four and a half stone and, owing to the shortage of eating disorder beds in the hospital, Susanne was admitted to a private clinic in 1995. At first, everything was progressing well. As a family we were invited to family meetings, but after a while Susanne began to self harm. Around this time in 1996 her consultant Dr A hinted that the cause could be the result of sexual abuse. He then forbade Susanne any contact with her family. At this time we were told it was to enable Susanne to become more independent.

One morning in July 1997 at 7am the doorbell rang. My husband, John, answered the door to find two detectives. The senior one accused him of committing acts of sexual abuse. John was escorted to the local police station. Police officers searched our home, and further officers questioned Julie, our younger daughter, at her home. After being detained for about eight hours John was driven home by one of the officers and told not to be unduly worried about the allegations. The police soon realised that Susanne's 28-page statement contained many inaccuracies, and parts appeared to have been copied from the book *The Courage to Heal*.

Dr A would not accept that the Crown Prosecution Service was of the opinion that there was no case to answer. He obtained an injunction forbidding John to have any contact with Susanne, and suggested that John should employ the services of a solicitor. This he did. The senior investigating officer telephoned the solicitor recruited by Dr A, to inform her that the allegations were false. Meanwhile, Dr A continued to pressurise myself and Julie to corroborate the statement written by Susanne.

During Dr A's vacations, Susanne would withdraw her statement and allegations, but on his return, contact with the family was terminated again. In the spring of 1998 John and I were invited to the clinic to state our concerns to an eminent professor, who was investigating our situation. At around this time Dr A was relieved of his duties at the clinic. Susanne was assigned a new consultant, Dr B. Susanne was encouraged to resume contact with the family, and after several consultations with John and myself, was discharged from the clinic and returned to live with us.

In our case, Susanne has 'returned' to our family. However, this ordeal, which lasted two years, did profoundly affect us all. The healing process has taken many years, aided by the good work of a psychologist of some repute who has helped Susanne to come to terms with her problems.

CLARE

Clare's parents are working as Pastors in the USA when she alleges her father abused her as a child. Dismissed from his job on the basis of the allegations he returns to the UK to face charges, all of which are later dropped by police.

In March 2005 we were serving as Pastors in a church in eastern USA, having left the UK to enter full time ministry at the end of 2001. Our youngest daughter was with us and studying at university in America, while our two elder daughters were both living in the UK where the eldest worked as a hairdresser while the middle daughter, Clare, worked on the staff at a large church in East Anglia.

Our world was shattered when we received a telephone call to say that our middle daughter had been undergoing counselling for the past two years and had alleged in December 2004 that I, her father, had sexually abused her from the ages of four to nine culminating in a violent rape act when she was around nine years old.

Needless to say it was devastating and we went through weeks of torment of trying to understand what could have gone on, as I knew I had not done any such thing. Together we battled on for three months trying to get to the bottom of what had happened, but given the nature of our work it was clearly impossible to just carry on regardless. Following many conversations with the leaders of the church in both England and America, I was dismissed from my post and forced to return to England, determined to face the accusations, put the record straight by involving the police if necessary, and return to the US to continue my work there.

While at the airport waiting to board our flight to the UK we received an email informing us that in the light of our impending return our daughter had gone to the police and that we were to contact them as soon as we returned.

I called the officer handling the case the very next day and arranged to present myself to the local police station for questioning. In the meantime I visited the BFMS and received great support and encouragement from Madeline who was able to shed some light on a number of issues, and also introduced us to a solicitor who would accompany me to the police interview.

On arrival at the police station I was arrested and cautioned and then interviewed a number of times over the next seven hours, being placed in a cell between each interview for extended periods of time. I was able to give a totally honest and open account of myself and the police also interviewed my wife, who also gave them the same report.

I was bailed to reappear early October, but this was then put back to November, and then finally postponed until January 2006. A few days before the meeting I contacted my solicitor to check that the meeting was to go ahead, and he eventually called me back to tell me that the police had looked at the evidence and decided to drop all charges against me. They stated three primary reasons for this decision: the medical evidence did not match up; the witness statements did not support the allegations; they were particularly impressed with a photograph taken two years earlier with a picture of my daughter sitting on my lap with her arm around me and smiling, a picture that did not match up to the events she claimed had taken place 14 years earlier.

Although we have felt immense relief at the police decision it has highlighted to us that people will still believe what they want to, and people that we have served faithfully with over many years are still blinded by the seriousness of the allegations and unwilling to believe that we have told the truth from the very beginning.

Our hope and firm belief is that we will still be reconciled with our daughter and that she will receive the help she so desperately needs.

ZOE

After reading 'The Courage to Heal', Zoe tells her parents that, according to her therapist, she had been abused as a child by her father. Zoe even admits she can't actually remember the incidents of abuse herself.

In 1992 our family entered a nightmare which took almost 10 years to resolve – and we are one of the few families to reach such a happy conclusion after years of totally unnecessary heartbreak. We had a daughter and two sons in their early 20s, part of a close family and settled in the world. The previous year my mother died of cancer; my daughter and I nursed her through her final months in our home.

The death of her beloved granny hit our daughter hard and our family doctor took the common sense approach that time, family and friends would help her through. But she looked for more advice and another physician decided she needed 'someone to talk to'. Thus we heard the words 'analytical psychotherapist' for the first time.

We agreed to pay the substantial bills of this practitioner for a year and were invited to meet her ourselves. We were completely taken in by this seemingly charming and helpful person – later discovering that she had been working as a travel agent not long before.

She saw my husband and me, together and separately, and asked many extraordinary questions about our childhoods, our parents and medical histories. We had no idea what she had in mind. Our daughter was given *The Courage to Heal* to read, told to write down her dreams nightly and urged to look into her childhood medical records. Amid all this we were stunned when she said 'the fact that I had my tonsils removed at the age of nine is a clear sign that I was being abused by someone'.

One day Zoe calmly told my husband that, although she didn't remember it, according to her therapist she had been abused by him as a child. We were totally devastated. My husband said that he, too, didn't remember and would hardly have forgotten! Primed by the therapist's previous brainwashing, my daughter told her father that he was 'in denial'.

This was only the beginning of our family's agony. Our younger son, then 21, decided to see our daughter's therapist and he also started to believe everything she said. He never accused either of us of abuse but changed from being exceptionally caring and loving into a withdrawn, distant and unhappy young man. He soon went to live elsewhere and any contact was infrequent, unfriendly and decidedly hostile. Our daughter went to live in her college, so, in one fell swoop, I lost my mother and two of my much-loved children.

We live in a small village and, at that time, ran a business which required us to present a cheerful face to the world. We maintained our busy lives, in spite of endless sleepless nights and heartbroken days when it was hard to keep going. Thankfully we discovered, joined and gained immense support from the BFMS.

Family festivals and Christmas were a complete nightmare. One of the worst times was when we learned that our daughter and her partner were about to make us grandparents. As she hadn't told us herself we expected never to see the baby.

Initially we decided not to tell anyone of our terrible situation but, gradually, we told our very closest family and friends on the understanding that they would not tell anyone else. We felt that, if our children ever came back, it would be easier for them if they were not known to have made accusations against their parents. The amazing support of our friends became absolutely vital to our survival during this dark period.

Miraculously a thread of contact with our children remained. Despite everything, birthday and Christmas cards were exchanged, though presents, and any other contact, were taboo. Our loyal son overcame his own suffering to maintain regular contact with his siblings, hoping to be a bridge between us and them. This indeed was exactly what happened and we are eternally grateful for his love and support.

Maybe it was because the link was not completely severed that, completely out of the blue in December 2001, our daughter wrote asking if she could meet me with her baby. It was an unbelievably emotional occasion for us both when we met again. To start with, we had to progress very slowly, and it was some while before our son started to get in touch again. We have never discussed the events of the previous years, but we accept that unconditional love for our children is what matters, and we now have a wonderful and united family with young grandchildren, all of whom we see on a regular basis, even for family holidays!

As far as the therapist is concerned, we discovered that even as she 'treated' our children, she was under supervision by her professional body having been found guilty of malpractice in another case. It seems she may no longer be practising 'recovered memory' techniques, but she was not struck off.

CHARLES

The BFMS proves a constant source of support for Charles' parents, after he accuses them of abuse following several years of 'regression therapy'.

Let me first of all say that as parents, we were not 'perfect'. Who is? We were an average middle class family. While we did experience marital problems when our three children were in their mid-to-late teens, I am absolutely certain that childhood was a happy time. Which makes the counsellor's approach described later all the more mystifying.

The insidious process of the estrangement from us of our eldest son, Charles, during his 20s, at first puzzled and later dismayed my wife and me. The reverberations continue, though we are struggling from despair towards normality. From early childhood, he seemed to be enjoying life to the full. We saw a lot of him and shared many common interests.

He developed a long and deeply emotional relationship with an Australian girl. I am sure he was never happier than during this period in his life. With the benefit of hindsight it is not unreasonable to suggest that the start of the problem can be traced back to the point when this relationship ended and he quickly met another girl and they married.

He seemed reasonably happy at first but it was as the young family began to increase that Charles began to experience difficulties. He also had financial difficulties and serious problems at work, though we did not know that at the time. He had four children. Things were not perfect with the first child, but did not raise any alarm bells. After the second and third birth we found Charles to be distancing himself from us; even aggressive. Around the time that the fourth arrived we found ourselves rejected by him. At some point – we do not know when – he had contacted a practitioner of 'regression therapy', a process that involved his undergoing therapy on a regular, weekly basis for several years.

As accounts of alleged cruelty proliferated and 'progressed' from quite innocuous events to serious allegations back to the age of two years we made our first contact with the BFMS and experienced the first cool touch of sanity in an increasingly bizarre situation. The society's help has been invaluable.

In the year 2000 we went to visit him, hoping for some kind of normal discussion but there was no reasoning with him. It was as if he had become someone else. What followed we now know to be a classic 'hate your father, pity your mother' consequence of regression therapy related to me so often by many other BFMS members. He ordered me not to move or interrupt and launched a savage diatribe of resentment, abuse and accusation, blaming all his current problems on his parents and his childhood – again typical of the experiences related to me by other parents. All this stemmed from his sessions with the therapist. The experience was utterly devastating and my wife was often in tears. I was given medication for depression. It seemed as if he was trying to insert a wedge between us, his parents, encouraging his mother to hate me. It took almost two years before we began to regain some enjoyment from life.

After some investigation we discovered that the so-called 'college' of which the therapist is a 'graduate' bases its teaching on the belief that within everyone there are memories of everything that has ever happened – right back to birth and within the womb – and that with the help of psychotherapy they can be recovered. In one 'case history' reported on the college's website, the therapist claims to have helped his client (a woman) 'remember' 13 instances of abuse within the womb. Another even offers counselling in cases of alien abduction. In order to 'graduate' and start practising, students undergo four weekends of training for a fee of several hundred pounds. Follow-up courses are offered, but none lasts for more than a few weekends. No direct, case-by-case supervision is provided once the 'graduate' starts practising his or her new-found 'skills' on the unsuspecting client.

What mystified us, until we knew more, was that the therapist concentrated solely on our son's happy, early childhood, completely ignoring what we admit was not an ideal family life during his late teenage years, or his traumatic recent and current problems. It seems that the suffering was made infinitely worse by the form of therapy innocently chosen in response to his problems and by the therapist's total failure to exercise a 'duty of care' towards his client's family. Had he consulted a GP, he might have been prescribed short-term, Cognitive Behavioural Therapy treatment which may have, at least, prevented a bad situation being made a hundred times worse.

At last there is some light at the end of the tunnel. My wife and I have visited our son and daughter-in-law. Hopefully, we have embarked on the long process of rebuilding our relationship.

SARAH

Sarah accuses her father of sexually abusing her as a child. She gives no details but with the help of her therapist she is led to believe it's the only explanation for the problems in her life.

My husband and I have piles of photos and jolly letters revealing Sarah as a happy, loving child, though she had a number of health problems, unlike her robust elder sister, Anna. She caught every bug going and welcomed the chance to stay home from school but she loved church and was remarkably devout, even acquiring housemaid's knee from praying.

In her teens, taller than her contemporaries, she preferred adult company, becoming involved with a coterie of women church workers.

She was not afraid to voice irritation with her family but this all seemed normal. When away she wrote us long, loving letters.

Despite glandular fever in the sixth form, her excellent A Levels enabled her to read for a Theology degree. She invited us often to visit her. Our home was open house to her friends.

In 1989, her finals year, she went down with myalgic encephalomyelitis and scraped a 2:2. Many job applications were unsuccessful and she came home to live, very depressed. She failed several driving tests, which she blamed on her father's tactlessness at crucial moments. She disliked her job with the local council. Various boyfriends either paired off with other girls or declared themselves 'gay'. By now she was hardly speaking to us.

Sarah accepted a job back at her university but did not enjoy it. She was also at this time advised to apply for ordination. Though opposed to women priests I tried to support her. At the selection weekend she clammed up and was told she needed counselling. After failing to enter the church she realised that she was probably running away from a vocation to become a nun. Eventually she was accepted by a convent but this coincided with her appointment to the staff of a boarding school. We heard little more about her vocation.

As she was now a short drive from us, we assumed we would see more of her. Before moving there she had been seeing a Christian therapist with whom she said she had constantly discussed her sister. Now she moved on to a new practitioner and became increasingly elusive, making many excuses to avoid family occasions. We saw her about five times in four years. At one very strained formal meal in her school flat she pointed out a book. The title meant nothing at the time but I believe now it was *The Courage to Heal*.

In 1997, desperate, we left a message asking to be allowed to drop in, just for a cup of tea. She replied that she was depressed and barely coping. I was terrified she was suicidal. We wrote loving supportive letters but from then on saw nothing of her.

Suddenly, in March 2000, she told us of her engagement. Anna, in slight contact with her, warned us she was probably going to ask an ex-monk to give her away. I wrote saying we would not attend other than in a parental role. In June Sarah replied, accusing my husband of a 'wrong' sexual relationship with her as a child. She had been led to see it was the only explanation of her problems. Her professional psychotherapist had 'held my hand as I began to cope with my reality'.

We strenuously refuted her charges and offered alternative causes of her illness, in particular a family tendency to depression. She ignored our letters and cut herself off from all her family, including Anna, and former friends. In October 2004 a solicitor's letter threatened us with a court order against any attempt to contact her directly or through her friends or her husband's family.

We have learnt that she is house mistress at a boarding school and has a young daughter. It is more than eight years since we saw her.

PRISCILLA

A homeopath and 'The Courage to Heal' help Priscilla to believe that her physical ailments stem from long-repressed memories of sexual abuse. She calls her father to tell him that she needs to see him because of what she has 're-remembered'. Puzzled and apprehensive, he drives for several hours to meet her.

On Thursday afternoon I arrived at Priscilla's London flat, and the door was opened by a young woman whom I didn't know who introduced herself as Lena. She said that she was there to help Priscilla and she ushered me into the front room of the flat. In the bay window there was a raised dais and my daughter was sitting there, in a lotus position like a little Buddha. In the centre of the room was a large chair, and she motioned me to sit in the chair. Lena came in behind me, shut the door, and sat by it, like a guard.

Priscilla then said something like: 'I want you to listen to what I'm going to say and what I'm going to read to you, and when I'm finished, I shall get up, leave this room, go into the garden, and you are to leave the house. I don't want you to say anything. I don't want you to ask any questions. I just want you to listen to me.'

She then started reading from a handwritten statement. The opening was a sort of preamble describing how she'd had a poisoned life up until now, that she'd managed to strip away the poisoned outer layers of her personality, and she'd been able to discover her true inner self. She then explained the reasons she had these poisoned layers and proceeded to tell me about the 'sexual abuse' that she had been subjected to when she was nine months old, two years, four years, eight... It was all a complete shock to me.

I went numb. I could not believe what I was hearing. I remember thinking: 'This is not real, this couldn't be happening.' Priscilla moved into a second part to talk about the compensation she wanted to help her overcome the pain and suffering the supposed abuse had caused her. She needed psychotherapy for two more years. She needed a safe place to live. And at the end of each item, she gave a monetary figure. At the end, she said: 'So the total is £70,000,' but quickly added, 'I'll settle for £50,000.' I hasten to add I never paid her any money, other than to help pay for psychotherapy that I thought would help her.

Then Priscilla read out a letter from a Davina Anivad, her homeopath. I subsequently got a copy of it, so I will read part of it to you. It is addressed, To Whom It May Concern. 'As a professional practitioner, I wish to state that all Priscilla Brightwell's symptoms, whether physical, mental or psychological, are consistent with her being a survivor of father/daughter rape, over a continued period of time. I have a great deal of experience in working with people who have been abused as children, and sadly Priscilla is one of them ... The healing only starts to begin with the re-surfacing of the memories.' Finally Priscilla read the end of the letter: 'The abusive father, who could face many long years in prison, should seek help for himself and not deny the damage he has done to his daughter, whose safety was in his hands. He must not expect forgiveness from her.'

This whole scene lasted about half an hour. It seemed like an eternity, though. The only other thing I said was at the end. I said: 'Those things didn't happen, Priss.'

I left Priscilla's flat literally in a state of shock. I got in my van and drove round the corner to a phone box and rang up Rachel, my youngest daughter, who lived nearby. (My oldest daughter, Mary, was married and living abroad, so she wasn't part of this). I said: 'Rachel, I just had the most disastrous meeting with Priscilla,' and she said: 'Yes, I know. And I believe her.' So that was sort of a double blow. I haven't seen Rachel or Priscilla since.

When I got home I contacted my ex-wife, Hannah, and arranged to meet her. Of course, she knew all about it. These accusations had been coming out for weeks, apparently. Hannah and I agreed we would seek proper therapeutic help for her. So we found a well-recommended therapist in London, Stephanie Brent, at the London Institute.

However, I soon became very concerned that this woman had not made a proper diagnosis of their problems. She was treating them for the wrong disease. She was treating them as if they were victims of real childhood sexual abuse. There was some pretty acrimonious correspondence between us which got nowhere. I was so outraged that she should call my daughters my 'ex-family'. In the end, I stopped paying for them to have therapy.

A year later, an acquaintance in America sent me a copy of an early False Memory Syndrome Foundation Newsletter. It was a revelation. It was the first ray of sunshine through dark clouds. I could clearly see that my daughters had been clobbered by this new seemingly American phenomenon called False Memory Syndrome. Naively and probably stupidly, I thought I had only to show Priscilla and Rachel the evidence of FMS and they would quickly see that they had become victims of it. I had not taken into account that I was not dealing with rational people. I sent them a copy of the newsletter and Melody Gavigan's early Retractor Newsletter. Then all hell broke loose.

Priscilla called and left a message on my answering machine. Her words tumbled out onto the tape in a bitter torrent. To me, the most important thing that comes across from that tape is that she really believes that those things happened to her and has integrated it into her personality. If you met her, you wouldn't think that anything was wrong. She would seem perfectly normal. It's really frightening.

After a while, Priscilla wrote: 'Now Rachel has remembered too, but it's different.' I never discovered what the difference was exactly. So I now have two daughters out there, seemingly believing that I did those terrible things to them, when of course I didn't. The whole thing is so stupid and implausible. There doesn't seem to be much I can do about anything. I honestly don't know how to help them realise that their nightmare images never actually happened.

This is an edited version of the Harold Brightwell story that first appeared in the British edition of *Victims of Memory* by Mark Pendergrast.

ADAM & DIANE

Out of the blue Adam and Diane's parents receive letters accusing them of shocking abuse and blaming them for everything that has gone wrong in their children's lives. The correspondence has clearly been influenced by 'The Courage to Heal'.

Almost a year ago now we received from our son and daughter, out of the blue, the most shocking and devastating letters imaginable. They were accusing both of us of sexual abuse against them as children, blaming us for things going wrong in their lives and, what is more, claiming that we had shown signs of attempting to put our grandchildren into situations of abuse. They forbade us to make any further contact with them or the children, not even for birthdays or Christmas. They had been referred to the police, who had advised them to cease contact with us 'because the safety of the children is paramount'.

Both these initial letters had given the name and number of a certain police officer at a nearby police station if we needed further information. We phoned him immediately. No question of interviewing us had been considered nor did the Child Protection Officer wish to speak to us now. It was not necessary, we were told, to be questioned and yet this was such a grave matter on which our life's purpose depended and on which such a cruel judgment was to be pronounced.

So our lives had been shattered by terrible, false, outrageous accusations which had no verification and without us being even able to deny them. The Child Protection Officer could not or would not enlighten us as to what had prompted such a sudden onslaught which was forbidding us from seeing our four adorable granddaughters. We

51

were beside ourselves with anger, confusion, frustration, helplessness and grief. Further letters were exchanged, still making the same blinkered and irrational accusations. We emailed several times pleading for a meeting or a discussion, hoping to achieve a change of heart, all without any success at all.

We have told several family members and close friends what was happening and they were all very supportive. We felt we needed a vote of confidence in our innocence. Also it seemed too big a thing to conceal from friends who knew us well. All were amazed and mystified that our charming son and daughter could treat us in this way. Some wrote letters of protest but these were either ignored, returned or refuted.

All this had followed immediately after a holiday, spent with each family separately, and a year after our daughter had spent a number of weeks with us in our house whilst their own was being extended. Thus we were living closely together, as one family, and wonder now what could have been so misjudged during those times, or how they could think so badly of us.

We have never claimed to be perfect parents and admit to problems in our relationship in earlier days, but have tried to be helpful, fair and loving grandparents and parents, often helping financially and otherwise.

In our search for help we spoke to our daughter's GP, who rang in response to my desperate letter. We respected her need for confidence but she did say she had tried to encourage our daughter to 'see things from a different viewpoint' from the one she had. We knew about her needing anti-depressants from time to time and seeing a therapist. Also she studied psychology at A Level. We have now begun to wonder if these things had induced her actions.

At our GP's suggestion we consulted an eminent psychiatrist. He was the first person to mention 'false memory syndrome' which we were quick to follow up. This brought our attention to the book *The Courage to Heal*, parts of which clearly influenced some of the emails we had received e.g.: 'What went wrong in my childhood? Why do I have no real memories before the age of eight? I have a few flashes of memory during this time. Why has this period of my life been almost wiped out of my mind? Something so bad must have happened for this to have occurred.'

Compare this with the section headed: 'But I don't have any memories' (p. 81 *The Courage to Heal*): 'But I had to ask myself, "Why would I be feeling all of this? Why would I be feeling all this anxiety if something didn't happen?" If the specifics are not available to you then go with what you've got.'

Our son is a converted Muslim and his wife, also a Muslim, had studied psychology and we realise she could have easily been influenced by such a book also.

Our daughter could have been a victim of 'false memory syndrome'. She and her sister-in-law seem to have encouraged each other in their ideas.

The Citizens Advice Bureau suggested we all consult a mediator so we and the two couples saw her separately three times over many weeks but finally it was claimed that specific points had not been answered by us so the results were extremely unhelpful and disappointing. Since then though we have realised that a family therapist might have been more equipped to deal with our problem but the moment for our children's co-operation had passed.

Our third and youngest child is in America, the one who was most difficult and commanded most attention, both as a child and as an adult. We wondered about sibling rivalry all along as there has been no contact for many years. The older daughter sensed my disapproval of this as I expected her to make the effort. I believe she has resented me because of this, although I have not felt critical of her for some years.

As for our son, we wonder if religion has played a part in his and his wife's feelings towards us. Being quite strict Muslims, perhaps they find it easier to cut off from us, rather than endure our 'western ways'.

We have lost confidence, focus and self esteem and at times have been unable to help each other, putting painful criticism and self-analysis upon ourselves and this has caused a great strain on our marriage.

Meanwhile we try to keep busy, appreciate the good friends and supportive family who are helping us to survive and pray that one day there will be a reconciliation between us.

SUSAN

While attending a family counselling session, Susan accuses her father of sexual abuse. The allegations devastate her dad and lead to the break up of the family.

My daughter Susan (now 25) an only child, had, I thought, a normal upbringing. She was lucky enough to be healthy, intelligent, good at sports and popular. My wife and I had good jobs and Susan had what could be described as a comfortable life. Above all she was dearly loved and cherished by everyone. I was often abroad but that seemed to emphasise our love for each other, she was a Daddy's girl and I doted on her.

At the age of 15 she developed anorexia and latterly bulimia. We all had a torrid time. She was in and out of institutions and hospitals. There were three suicide attempts. To her credit she kept studying and achieved excellent GCSE results and a string of A Levels. She saw numerous therapists and occasionally was medicated. My wife and I did all we could to help and explored all avenues. With hindsight we should not have listened to all the advice, some of it I'm convinced now was seriously flawed. Although not entirely recovered she attended university but struggled without the required support. Eventually under her own initiative she took time out from her studies and attended a residential tertiary care establishment for a period of 18 months. It was during this time that she began to withdraw from, initially, both my wife and I but eventually just me.

In September of 2003 I was out of the country for two weeks and upon my return the bomb was dropped. My wife told me that for a few weeks she and Susan had been attending family counselling sessions together and that at one of these meetings it was stated that I had seriously sexually abused my daughter. My wife said she had to believe the accusations and after 28 years of marriage left me immediately. I was spared the details.

I visited our family GP and Susan's psychologist who were both very supportive and said it would all come to nothing and that any specific details would be easy to refute. However, they both advised that I seek the assistance of a solicitor, as I did not know if I was to be charged. For a period I was terrified and really did not know what to do for the best. My close friends helped enormously and were always there for me.

Out of the blue eight months later came a letter from Susan saying that the allegations were untrue. A week or two after that came a letter from the family counselling group asking if I would be willing to attend a series of meetings with Susan. Of course I did and although they were extremely difficult at first, we were getting back on track. We went out for meals and she visited home where we met up with some old acquaintances. We phoned each other and exchanged Christmas gifts. She successfully completed her degree. It was good to look forward and not to dwell on all the bad experiences.

Unfortunately, a year after the meetings started they began to break down and culminated in a letter from Susan once again cutting off all ties. This left me just waiting for something to happen. My beautiful, intelligent, humorous daughter was out there somewhere doing something and I wasn't part of her life. It was a devastating position to be in.

But there is light at the end of the tunnel. My daughter recently re-established contact with me once again. Christmas cards have been exchanged and we now telephone each other. We are also planning to visit each other's homes.

I live in hope that she will continue to want to have me in her life. I still love and cherish her and will until the day I die.

SIMON

Simon accuses his mother of acting in a sexually inappropriate way with him when he was 13, just before his father died. The accusations leave her estranged from the rest of her family.

My son Simon was in his late 20s in a respected profession and married when, out of the blue, he telephoned to accuse me, his mother, of having acted in a sexually inappropriate way with him just before his father died when he was 13. He stated that he did not wish to see or speak to me again. Supported by his wife he has since refused all form of contact. This totally untrue accusation was and remains quite devastating. Only a month or so previous to this we were the best of friends, our life was normal.

The accusation was made during the initial phase of an acute mental illness requiring hospitalisation. He had suffered a previous episode that also required hospitalisation about five years previously, which was possibly precipitated by multiple stress factors including studying for exams. He had delusions in this episode. Was this accusation a delusion in the second illness to which credence was given and has it become a false memory that he has clung to as a reason for his illness? I was widowed when he was going through puberty. Has he retrospectively enlarged and distorted into fantasy some actual, innocent memory? So many questions, so few answers and with no communication how can one move forward?

The accusation was in 2003. I had been a widow for 13 years during which time I had seen Simon and his elder brother, Timothy, through public school. Simon went on to university and Tim became a successful businessman. After the false allegation Timothy initially kept in contact with his brother and me but he refused to discuss the issue with me. He has been facing a conflict of loyalties between his brother and me, which has recently come to a head resulting in his continuing to see his brother but not having contact with me. He seems to be giving more credence to Simon's accusations. He is divorced and does not now wish his child to stay with me in spite of the fact that she has regularly done so all her life. The shock of my second child seeming to believe the falsehood and severing contact just heightens the feeling of injustice and bewilderment. I did not believe things could get any worse.

Nothing could have prepared me for what has happened. Any sexual abuse towards a child is shocking and inexcusable and yes it does happen. However, I now know that false allegations are also sometimes made by those whom one loves the most and these allegations can and do cause terrible pain and devastation to the whole family and beyond. My son was a loving, well-balanced, happy boy. He grew into an independent intelligent successful man and in spite of his two short periods of illness he seems to be working and functioning well.

Why this accusation? I truly don't understand. I have tried to make sense of the situation but there is no sense in it. There are no winners only losers. I spend many sleepless nights just hoping and praying that this ghastly nightmare will one day cease. Perhaps Simon will wake up to the truth one day and have the strength of character to admit to it. I think the thing that hurts the most is that he could believe that I could be capable of hurting him in such a way. Everyday is now an uphill struggle for me and I long to see my children and grandchildren and be a family once again.

HEATHER

After a long period of therapy Heather accuses her father of having sexually abused her when she was a child. However, her 'memories' of the event are far from accurate.

More than 14 years ago my daughter Heather, then in her early 30s, accused me, her father, of having sexually abused her when she was a small child. This was after a long period of therapy which she had been persuaded to undertake by her husband. She is now divorced.

I am prevented, because of the ex-husband's objections, from meeting Heather's son, my grandchild, who is now 10 years old. In this the law is outrageously unjust to my daughter, my grandson and me. Heather, meanwhile, has come out of her nightmare and now recognises that her accusations arose out of something like brainwashing by her therapist who was influenced by the clinical fashion in the profession at the time. She has suffered a great deal in the process but we are in touch and get on well.

Meanwhile I soldiered on, determined not to let this business destroy me. I have had an eventful life, built up a successful business from nothing and was able to retire early to a new life overseas. Heather's mother and I parted many years ago (I have remarried) and it may be that the ups and downs of her earlier years contributed to the problems for which she sought help. I never molested her in any way but have come to believe that in everyday terms 'what goes round comes around'. The upheavals gave her grief and I got it back - that's how I see it.

Anyway, Heather did well in her education and qualified in her profession. I am thankful for that and things are coming together. It was a bombshell when her accusation landed and I tackled it head on.

I contacted the police, told them about it and said I would co-operate with them in any way. Things, however, never proceeded to a charge or a trial. The police told me that they could only investigate if there was a complaint made to them. Heather never did that. One of the officers also told me, 'We know all about low-lifes and that's not you Jack.'

One of Heather's 'memories' was of being carried downstairs by me from her room and then sexually assaulted.

We were living in a bungalow at the time.

It was nineteen months ago that I received the all important phone call from my daughter. We are now back in regular contact and she has fully retracted her accusations. Our relationship continues to go from strength to strength.

See p. 74 for Heather's story.

LUCY

After reading self-help literature and undergoing therapy Lucy accuses her father of abusing her as a child. Her parents turn to BFMS as they attempt to continue with their day-to-day lives.

We thought we were a normal family until our younger daughter, Lucy, in her late 20s, arrived on the doorstep to announce that my husband had raped her as a child and accused me of knowing and doing nothing about it. As my husband had actually never even smacked her, we were both bemused and devastated. However much we tried to discuss the situation with her it was as if her physical body was present in the room but her mind was that of a stranger and not our hitherto close and loving daughter.

In the subsequent days and weeks we found it extremely difficult to cope with normal living – each day became an uphill struggle with varying degrees of depression, despair and self-analysis as to where we had gone wrong and failed our daughter. Thankfully, we were introduced, at an early stage, to the British False Memory Society and Madeline and Donna were towers of strength in our darkest hours. We realised gradually that we were not on our own and this started to give us the will to investigate the situation more fully.

Lucy had always been the baby of the family and a complete 'home bird' but we were excited for her when she decided to move to London with her boyfriend and take a new job. Her new flat was in a basement and her boyfriend spent many days working away and we think that this contributed to her developing certain fears and phobias of a nervous nature. It appears that she was introduced to a New Age therapy which believes in regressive counselling and from these sessions and the reading of a book called *Breaking Free*, Lucy became convinced that she was sexually abused.[1] I have read this book and, quite frankly, anyone who reads it could probably tick many of the boxes and make the mistake of thinking that they were sexually abused as a child.

We have told a few close family and friends who, having known her all her life, actually laughed at the thought that either of us had abused Lucy.

Some people have tried to get in touch with her on our behalf but, sadly, she is obviously still brainwashed as she thinks that we are 'in denial' and that her life is now moving forward without us being involved. We did actually manage to speak to our son-in-law who said that she did not want any contact with us until she feels in control – whatever that means!

Perversely, Lucy has sent us Christmas, birthday and Mother's Day cards and most strangely, a Father's Day card, so we cling to the hope that somewhere in there, the old Lucy still exists.

We have an elder daughter, Sarah, who initially cut off relations with us for three months in sympathy with her sister and, although we suspect that she still thinks we are guilty, we have re-established a relationship of sorts with her.

---

[1] *Breaking Free: Help for Survivors of Child Sexual Abuse*, Ainscough, A., & Toon, K., Sheldon Press, 1993, new edition 2000.

ELEANOR

Police tell the sister of an accuser: 'If you cannot add to my case I don't need to speak to you. You have been abused but won't admit it!' Her father is dragged through the courts before it is ruled he has no case to answer.

My wife, Susan, and, I have three daughters: Margaret, Lorraine and Eleanor. Eleanor is the daughter from Susan's first marriage but was formally adopted by me when she was aged four. It was also Eleanor who was the first to accuse me.

Eleanor was born in 1962. In 1966 Margaret was born and in 1968 Lorraine arrived. I had a hectic, sometimes physically dangerous job, in a senior post with one of the public services. Susan and I worked hard to be a family and from the start I treated Eleanor as my own.

For different reasons, Eleanor and Lorraine had difficult childhoods but the first hint of the troubles we were to face came in 1991, when the girls were well into their twenties. A letter from our son-in-law, then living abroad with Eleanor, accused me of having sexually abused her. He threatened to go to the press with the allegation. We consulted a solicitor who wrote to him, not only denying his claims but warning that if he persisted with them we would go to the authorities.

Some months later Lorraine, then aged 23, told Susan she had witnessed me abusing Eleanor in the front room of our old home. She would have been just three years old at the time. Susan simply did not believe her. There were circumstances which would have made such clear perception impossible.

Lorraine was very ill as a small child with a condition which disabled her into her teens and beyond. She refused to speak to us about the allegations but some weeks later, after a rather strained visit, she told us that she did not want to see us ever again or be part of our family.

Thus we lived with the break-up of our family structure, for 13 years, until July 2004, when two detectives from the Child Protection Unit came to arrest me. Lorraine had alleged that I had abused her as well. I was questioned at length and released on bail.

Searching the net I found the BFMS website and contacted Madeline who was a great support to us and not only gave us relevant information but advice on what records, letters and other documents to search for.

It is only now, the Crown having decided that there is no case to answer, that I have the detachment to look back on all the stages of our lives that led to this tragedy for all five of us. Susan and I are so thankful that Margaret, our middle daughter, has been totally supportive throughout, giving us hope and encouragement. After all, she has lost her sisters, and her children their aunties and cousins.

In the wake of Lorraine's allegations the police went to Eleanor and asked her to prepare notes for an interview a couple of weeks later. I was called at home after this interview around 10.30pm and told there was a 'further complainant' and I would be required to attend the police station for a further interview. The detective did this without first contacting my solicitor. At the interview I was again cautioned and questioned about events ranging from 1964 to 1992, but in particular about rape, gross indecency and indecency to Eleanor between 1967 and 1984. I denied all these allegations.

I explained that because of behavioural problems from a very early age Eleanor had been under constant observation by school, grandparents, neighbours and the GP for many years. Also that there should be many records available as she was treated by a psychologist for about three and a half years, away from home, visiting various local authority residential units and assessment centres.

I asked the police why, if I had been abusing Eleanor, they thought I would allow her to be away from home in the care of professionals skilled at uncovering abuse. They told me I was covering my tracks! I am neither clever enough nor daft enough to think I could get away with such a thing.

When I next attended the police station I was told that I would be charged with two counts of rape, gross indecency and indecency. On hearing this I collapsed, passed out completely, and was admitted to hospital due to the stress. The strain on Susan and Margaret was immense.

Margaret contacted the officers as she had been told they needed to interview her and had failed to do so. When speaking to the lead Detective Constable she was told: 'If you cannot add to my case I don't need to speak to you'. Margaret challenged them and was told: 'You have been abused but won't admit it!' The officer later denied this conversation had taken place. Margaret recorded the time and date of her call.

In the ensuing months Susan, Margaret and I, with our solicitor, studied our girls' statements - observing that the notes Eleanor had prepared were written in two different hands. We also took a fine toothcomb to our family's past. Eleanor had exhibited behavioural problems from before I met her mother. There had been a troubled relationship with her birth father. There were many serious and worrying problems during her teens.

During the period covered by the accusations our home was open house to all and sundry, we had health visitors, district nurses, and physiotherapists, home tutors, our GPs and consultants, plus family visitors dropping in mostly without prior arrangement. How could I have carried out the abuse I was accused of without being discovered? There were also visits from education and welfare officers and workers assisting with Eleanor, who were free to drop in at any time and did so.

Lorraine had developed her illness at the age of two and spent seven months in hospital. At that point her condition was life-threatening but she pulled through. She remained subject to flare-ups and the need for more hospital visits throughout her childhood and adolescence. We did our best to include Eleanor and Margaret in her care, with the great assistance of my family, colleagues, friends and neighbours. I was told that at one stage in Eleanor's development the possibility of abuse by me was actively investigated as the cause of her behaviour and then ruled out.

Susan and I feel it is more than coincidental that the media were full of 'Recovered Memory' stories in the early 1990s - about the same time Eleanor was making her accusations. Also, we have discovered that while receiving treatment away from home, Eleanor became friends with a woman who had many problems, including a history of making false accusations against her father and other men - accusations which were all dismissed or withdrawn. We believe this is where these claims of Eleanor and Lorraine first began.

Hardest to accept has been the investigative procedure. It was biased, partial and not focused on uncovering the truth. The authorities, knowing Eleanor had had such a huge intervention from various agencies for most of her life, would not look for the records but rather dismissed them as irrelevant. Nor would they speak to some of the professionals still alive who could have given the lie to these claims.

Similarly they disregarded the total involvement of the health system in Lorraine's life.

While criminal proceedings against me have now ended - the Crown offered no evidence - the damage done by false accusations does not end when the police go away, as unfortunately, my family and I know only too well.

However, after all this time I refuse to just sit back and do nothing. I try to offer support and information to others who find themselves in the same situation and pass on the knowledge I have gained through my experience. I also take an active role in communicating with organisations and agencies that I have had dealings with, to make them aware of the pernicious, destructive nature of false memories.

ANN

A troubled child, Ann makes claims of incest against her father, claims that are supported by her psychiatrist. The police decide against taking action, but continued pressure from social services leads Ann's father to a nervous breakdown before his daughter finally retracts her allegations.

In August 1998 I was washing the family car when I was told my daughter, Ann, was at the door. She seemed bright and cheerful and had come, she said, for a purpose. She told me that she had really believed her accusations against me of sexual abuse during her childhood but had recently realised they were not true.

I put my arm around her and said it had all been a terrible nightmare for us. I was tearful and she kept saying she was so sorry. Thus ended more than eight years in which all our family had been under a dark cloud.

It was a very emotional day and I felt the pain draining out of me. Although it was a great delight to be reconciled with my daughter my thoughts were not so positive towards those misguided folk who poisoned her mind through their lack of knowledge and skill. As for those who mentally and emotionally assaulted me, I hope and pray that the truth will dawn on them.

Ann became ill in early 1990 at the age of 16, while preparing for her GCSEs. She had an older brother and three younger sisters. She was bright and caring towards others, was doing well at school and was very successful at sport but she was unhappy about our impending move to another area and probably had difficulties about her identity. She was disturbed and stopped eating and her condition became so severe that, with our encouragement, she entered an adolescent psychiatric unit in May 1990. We did not realise we were exposing her to many malevolent influences.

We attended family therapy sessions at the unit and Ann also joined a therapy group, known as the 'girls' group' which, we learned later, was for abused girls. I think now that her psychiatrist and her therapist had diagnosed her as 'abused' and suggested the group to her. Other girls in this group were very disturbed and during these sessions Ann's condition worsened. She absconded from the unit, cut herself and banged her head, often uncontrollably.

At a family therapy session her therapist, Moira, stated that Ann had been raped. Our daughter then ran from the room and although we were deeply shocked we were not allowed to see her again that day. The unit gave no details but the police contacted us later to give us Ann's account. By late July, however, the police officers told her that the rape story was falling down and suggested she was covering up for someone in her 'close family'. The suggestion upset Ann which, the sergeant claimed, proved that he was right. Soon afterwards Ann began to make claims of incest to her key worker, Jo, a newly qualified nurse. Jo took a special interest in Ann, to the point of breaking professional boundaries by giving her presents and making her a bridesmaid at her wedding. Ann said later that people at the unit kept on and on at her to say that her father had done something to her until she agreed, believing that she must have blocked it all out. After all, they were the experts so they should know.

Ann's claims were supported by her psychiatrist who ignored counter-claims about the force of suggestion from authority figures and adolescent peer pressure. Moira said it was her duty to believe her client. The result was that our daughter got worse and her recovery was set back for years. Ann did telephone to tell both of us that she had imagined the whole story and wanted to come home but the unit made it clear that if she decided to leave they would have her detained under the Mental Health Act. She was their prisoner and the retraction was temporary; a police statement was taken from Ann a day or two later, at the end of October 1990, and I was arrested and questioned. The devastating time became even worse.

I was accused of all sorts of sexual molestation, oral sex and full intercourse with Ann from the ages of seven to 14, all of which I denied because I had never, ever done or even thought of doing such things. At the same time a team from the police and social services checked the rest of the family at home and I think they were surprised to find nothing to be concerned about. Two policewomen interviewed my wife and told her she should believe Ann even though she did not.

Ann was re-interviewed in early January 1991 and we were informed that there would be no police proceedings.

I was greatly puzzled as well as upset. Ann appeared to be telling the truth but I knew she was not. As a result of my reading, especially Robert Temple's book on hypnosis, *Open to Suggestion*, I found that a person can sincerely believe untrue things, especially under certain conditions.[1] Ann's mental state and the conditions at the unit made her more and more suggestible. I argued that she had been accidentally brainwashed. All that I read then and have read since confirms to me that the way things were set up at the unit made this almost inevitable. This theory was dismissed by the unit professionals.

Social services persisted with their scrutiny, however, and in mid 1991 our children were placed on the Child Protection Register. This order remained in force for about 18 months as we did battle with a doctor appointed by social services. He was highly biased against us and failed to investigate the psychiatric unit. No-one from the health services side would accept that the developing problems were more to do with Ann and the unit than with the family. Social services, however, saw that the children at home were safe and secure and removed them from the Child Protection Register at the end of 1992. When the intense pressure of about three years was relaxed I had a nervous breakdown and was off work for about three months.

Meanwhile Ann continued to maintain the allegations and remained adamant in spite of our attempts to contradict her. Nevertheless we met as often as we could.

Ann only really started to settle down in mid-1992 after leaving the unit. She stayed in a hostel and then moved to a flat. Her progress included setbacks and we kept up a somewhat strained relationship with her and usually let her take the initiative in contacting us. Throughout this stressful period my wife was truly marvellous and showed powers of care and common sense that eluded many professional workers.

We saw Ann and the friend she lived with over Christmas 1997 but shortly afterwards we were visited by social workers. Ann was back in a psychiatric unit and her friend took the old accusations to the police. They took no further action but passed the complaint to our local social services who saw that all was well at home. Ann then wrote to say that she wanted no further contact with me and her mother. We replied as firmly as we could and assured her of our love and forgiveness. This was a great setback and we did not hear from her for several months. However, the Royal College of Psychiatrists had just published a report on false memories which showed, among other things, that patients with these problems were likely to suffer relapses.

We had always believed that a treatment based on untruth could not succeed. In August 1998 our faith was upheld when Ann came back to us. We learned later that over the previous few months Ann was having doubts about the allegations. When she realised that they were completely false and she had put me through hell she plucked up courage to inform the police and to tell me in person. The last eight years have been very positive in terms of family relationships and Ann's mental health and confirm that truth is a vital part of health and healing.

I believe that such hospital-created heartbreaks could be reduced if mental health workers had thorough training in the psychology of memory and the susceptibility of vulnerable clients to suggestion and influence.

[1] *Open to Suggestion*, Temple, R., Aquarian Press, 1989

HEATHER

*A retractor attributes her accusation to the influence of a 'truth drug' adminis-
tered by a Harley Street psychiatrist. After scrutiny of the 'memories' which led
to her accusation she realises that they are baseless and is reconciled with her
father.*

I am 43 years old, a qualified chartered accountant, now going
through a divorce and was estranged from my dad for 15 years.

I had been sent to a very famous Harley Street psychiatrist who
recovered some 'memories' for me which 'helped' me to understand
why I was so sexually inadequate for my partner. It is all too easy to
guess what comes next - it was all due to being sexually abused by my
dad. Even worse was that the psychiatrist 'helped' me realise that my
mum was bad too, as there is 'no such thing' as an innocent parent
where any type of abuse is concerned. It was not a great year for my
family in 1990/1, in fact worse than when my parents divorced in
1979.

But I got by. I married the partner who had found the nice psychiatrist - no wedding - just me, him, a cook and concierge as the wit-
nesses. I had a child but no thought for how he might miss having a
granddad - no thought for the granddad.

I managed to block the feelings for my dad and his wife. I felt
nothing, except when I got drunk when I could remember the nice
psychiatrist with the truth drug needle hanging off my wrist and all
the bad feelings that came with the memories. Then, about two or
three years ago, I really began to think and did a little research - the
truth drug is mind altering. My memories were really muddled: stairs
in the bungalow, the wrong dog in the house, my dad wearing pyjamas

and friends being the wrong age in the 'memories'. When I was eight or 12 they were often much older - the age that I was at the time when my 'memories' were recovered. At times I did feel as though I was going mad.

For a long time my mum always wanted to get in touch with dad, so when I said I wanted to see him she was pleased. My uncle would not give me dad's phone number as dad never asked about me and I would only upset his new life with my step-mum. It is true that dad never asked after me but my step-mum always did. So in January 2001 I wrote a letter to a solicitor that I thought he used but I didn't get a reply.

Finally, I left the nice man who had found me the nice psychiatrist and exploded in anger at my nice uncle, demanding that he give me my dad's phone number. Eventually, in June 2005, he left a message on my mobile with the number. What to do next I asked myself? It had been 15-odd years so what would another week matter? I had to make the call but how do you say sorry for falsely accusing your father - 'sorry for the lost years' and 'sorry you have never seen your grandson'. Well I found BFMS and, amazingly, so had my dad and stepmother but even communication from BFMS was too slow for me. So I just picked up the phone and dialled. I can't remember what I said but dad told me it was just great to hear from me and that he loved me and there was no need to say sorry. About a month after the first phone call I got in the car and drove down to see them both. It was great; I stayed three weeks and although we met as semi-strangers, in that time we really seemed to catch up on 15 lost years. We now call often and, oh boy, has my dad been able to help me with my life. I almost feel as if I'm using him because his understanding and knowledge of me is just so thorough and sometimes too ruthlessly honest. I know when I left my dad I made a void in my life that was painful. Now that void is filling with love, knowledge and honesty. Without my dad just accepting me as I am now and loving me now I would be totally lost again and I never want to be lost again. So for parents reading this, please just think of your child as being lost and lost people are frightened. My dad and stepmum made it so easy for me. Thanks to mum, dad and stepmum.

The Truth about 'Truth Serum'

Studies have revealed that during Sodium Amytal administration, patients often demonstrate a distorted sense of time, show memory disturbances, and have difficulty evaluating and selecting thoughts. In addition, under Amytal, patients' claims about details of their histories - events, places, names, dates - are untrustworthy. Further, investigations have shown that the drug also makes patients vulnerable to either accidental or deliberate suggestions from the interviewer. Finally, and most importantly, patients under Amytal fail to reliably discriminate between reality and fantasy.

Truth Serum & What Really Happened, Piper, A., 1994

MAXINE

Maxine relates her gradual realisation that the suggestions of her psychiatrist that she had been abused by her father as a child were false. Her discovery was too late to stop her being sterilised, on the advice of a psychologist, for fear that she might abuse any children of her own.

As I look back on my life, there are so many things I wish I could change, but there are also many things that I would not change. I am a survivor of false memory therapy. How could someone as young as I was get caught up in false memory syndrome? Actually, it was very easy. It was getting out of the false memory abyss that was more difficult.

I grew up in America and my difficulties started just before my high school graduation. There are conflicting stories from my parents as to what exactly occurred, but what I relate is told from my understanding of the facts. These facts were not told to me until recently when I was able to read depositions in a malpractice lawsuit that I brought against the hospital.

My reason for seeking therapy was depression that occurred shortly before my graduation. My records indicate that I was actually suffering from a physical and not a psychological problem, but the psychologist and psychiatrist to whom I turned did not take the time or effort to investigate any physical causes for my symptoms. Instead they jumped to a psychological diagnosis.

The events just before my graduation served as the basis for my 'therapy'. I was stressed about the graduation, perhaps in great part because my father wanted to attend. When I was in the first grade my parents had divorced and that was the last time I saw my father for 20

77

years. The key event that set the focus for my therapy was the fact that my dad wanted to come and see me graduate but my mother was strongly opposed. This created tremendous conflict at home and this period in my life was very sad for me.

I was hospitalised for the first time less than a month before my graduation and I remained so until some time afterwards. During this time my therapist alleged many horrific things about my father. I now believe that the 'flashbacks' and 'memories' of abuse I supposedly recovered were induced by my psychiatrist after he talked with my mother. My mother is the one who believed that I had been abused. Many of my supposed 'memories' closely corresponded to my mother's beliefs about what had occurred, I learned later from the papers in the lawsuit.

The doctors and therapists communicated what I said about my 'recovered memories' to my mother. She never told them or me that these things never happened. I was victimised and my father's name was ruined. To make matters worse, the legal records show that my doctors had been told there was no evidence to support their belief about me being sexually abused by my father.

I was hospitalised many times the next year and that was awful, but during this same time I met the man who was to be my husband, and that was wonderful. I married Brian that year. It is said that people have 20/20 vision in hindsight. As I look back, I realise my husband was trying to tell me something was not right with my therapy and my therapists. Unfortunately I did not listen to him. Instead I chose to listen to my mother, the therapists, and the doctors. This mistake led to my temporary separation from my husband, but fortunately we were able to overcome this problem. I realised that I needed to make some changes in my life.

I stopped my contact with my mother, I changed doctors, and I decided to research what they were saying to me. Slowly the truth came to the surface; I had been told a fabrication. But why would my doctors and my mother do such a thing? I believe the doctors and therapists knowingly or unknowingly were influenced by the easy availability of insurance money. I believe my mother was caught up in emotional revenge and that she saw herself as a heroine who was saving me from the terrible person of my father.

Two people helped me back to reality. The saving forces in my life were my husband and my family doctor. Both challenged the truth of the therapy in which I had come to believe. Shortly after I recognised that my memories were false, I filed suit and started to piece my life back together. I have much to be thankful for; in addition to the support from my husband and doctor, I am thankful that I have had the opportunity to meet my father twice.

Unfortunately, my mother continues to be greatly upset that I have established contact with my dad and that makes a very difficult situation for me. I hope that one day we can talk about it and that she is able to see the role that she played in my nightmare and maybe even apologise. I can't help but feel that if she had done something to prevent the falsehoods from spreading, I would have not have been sterilised. One psychologist who was treating me told me that I had to get my tubes tied because I had been abused. The reasoning is that since I had been abused, I would abuse any child that I might have. If that had not happened, my mother would be enjoying grandchildren now.

I hope that by sharing this story I can prevent more abuse in therapy. I hope I can stir an awareness of how this type of therapy destroys relationships. I hope I can alert people to the harm that can result when therapists believe they know more about a patient's life than she does.

Who would think that a high school graduation could be the catalyst of such a bizarre experience? How wonderful that with the love and support of my husband, I have been able to join the real world.

Repression - a theory,
not a fact

Everyone is aware of the frustration of inaccessible memories, when we cannot recall something that we wish to do, like finding a name, or recalling an event from childhood that must have occurred, or when we fail to recognise a person who appears totally unfamiliar until he proceeds to recount to us when and where we met. Much less familiar is the phenomenon of remembering something to which we have *no* right - because it is for an event that never occurred.

There is now abundant laboratory evidence for the creation of such false memories (for an academic review, see *The Science of False Memory*).[1] They are relatively easy phenomena to generate if a powerful, and repetitive suggestion is made by an authoritative and persuasive mentor, and especially if it is within the context of a compelling wider framework. Clearly false memories can play a dangerous role in witness testimony and other claims for the recall of non-existent or seriously distorted events. The most serious examples, perhaps, are accusations of severe sexual abuse that never occurred, although fervently believed by the accuser. A person who is the target of such an accusation can have his or her life deeply and irrevocably damaged. It is not only fractured families who emerge, but tragically fractured and shattered individuals. And subsequently, if the truth finally emerges, damage can rebound upon the accuser.

The most common context within which these emerge is in forms of therapy based on the tenet that many problems of everyday life, both physical but especially psychological, have developed because of childhood abuse, a view propounded in books such as *The Courage to*

Heal[2] and other treatises. If the client in such a therapeutic regime cannot remember any such abuse, the claim is that it must have been deeply repressed and made inaccessible, but with appropriate therapy the memory can be 'recovered.' And, indeed, clients can come honestly to be persuaded that the recovered memory must be true even if it is not.

There is no solid experimental evidence, as such, for the core tenet of this approach, the repression of traumatic memories. Of course, it is not an easy matter to investigate in the laboratory, and the matter has been controversial for over 100 years. But two Harvard psychiatrists, Drs. Harrison Pope and James Hudson, carried out a determined and thorough search some 10 years ago of the published literature for reliable, acceptable evidence of the repression of memories of sexual abuse, and failed to find a single example or study that stood up to rigorous test.[3] (See articles about their research and its implications in *The Times*, March 16 and April 11, 1995; see, also, a review by another Harvard psychologist, Richard J. McNally, 'Science and falsehood of traumatic amnesia').[4] Repression is a theory, not a fact. Theory aside, there is ample evidence that, on the contrary, those who have suffered traumatic stress have the opposite problem - it is not that they cannot remember but that they have trouble in forgetting the trauma.

By now there is an accumulation of large numbers of examples of accusations of childhood abuse having been made for which evidence subsequently demonstrated that they could not have happened. It is rare for anyone who has been the object of such a false accusation easily to recover from such an experience, especially if made by a loved one, even if the charge is demonstrated to be false. These are compound fractures that may never heal. Childhood abuse is, of course, a dire problem not to be underestimated. But adult abuse by fervent accusers, often of a crusading vigilante nature, based on events that never occurred, is a life-shattering experience.

Professor Larry Weiskrantz, FRS.
Emeritus Professor of Psychology, University of Oxford

[1] *The Science of False Memory*, Brainerd, C.J., Reyna, V.F., Oxford University Press. 2005

[2] *The Courage to Heal*, Bass, E., Davis, L., Vermilion, first edition in UK 1990 (reprinted on numerous occasions up to 2002).

[3] Pope, Jr, H.G., and Hudson, J.I., 'Can Memories of Childhood Sexual Abuse be Repressed?' *Psychological Medicine*, 1995, v.25, p. 121-126

[4] McNally, R.J., 'Science and falsehood of traumatic amnesia' *Clinical Psychology: Science and Practice*, 2004. 11, 29-39

Epilogue

It is my hope, as the editor of the stories told here, that they will be a catalyst for new beginnings: happy ones, for the families who have taken part and, perhaps, for thousands of others.

There are almost 2,000 families on the books of the BFMS and maybe many more who are not known to us or to whom we are not known. I am grateful to those who have written or related their stories to me. It can be very painful calmly to gather one's composure and coolly face the hard facts and consequences of false accusation.

As well as an implicit appeal to the 'powers that be' to look hard at their assumptions about recovered memory accusations, this book is also, in effect, a letter to its writers' children, who often return unopened whatever arrives by Royal Mail.

The depth of society's condemnation of the sexual abuse of children, which we share completely, is also a measure of the agony of the falsely accused, as they face the effective loss of a loved family member – an experience frequently compared to that of bereavement.

As this book shows, eating disorders, depression and self harm are prominent among the conditions which are commonly assumed to arise out of sexual abuse. Devout believers in 'recovered memory' or 'buried trauma' are able to create many others. Sadly, it seems, clinicians have made their diagnosis of abuse out of something like blind faith in the theory.

Since the late 1980s a major, possibly seminal influence in the development of 'recovered memory' treatments has been the self-help book *The Courage to Heal* which famously says: 'If you think you were abused and your life shows the symptoms then you were.' It also urges those who don't remember abuse to act 'as if they have been'.[1]

Fractured Families

It has been described by Claire Curtis-Thomas MP, chairman of the all-party group on abuse investigations, as 'one of the most dangerous self-help books ever written'. Despite protests, however, it is regularly included on reading lists. The personal experiences documented here highlight the dangers.

The doctrine, maybe even the sexual politics, which are within the recovered memory movement, stalk the land still, endangering many more innocent families: families like those who stoically and sadly tell their stories here.

As collator of these accounts I offer my thanks to the staff of the BFMS for the design and presentation of this book's contents.

Norman Brand

[1] *The Courage to Heal*, Bass, E.; Davis, L., Vermilion London 1997 (p. 22 & p. 82)

Further Reading

Aldridge-Morris, R., *Multiple Personality: An Exercise in Deception*, Lawrence Erlbaum Associates, 1991

Brainerd, C.J., Reyna, V.F., *The Science of False Memory*, Oxford University Press, 2005

Burgoyne, W., *Counselling or Quackery?*, pabd.com, 2004

Campbell, T.W., *Smoke and Mirrors: The Devastating Effect of False Sexual Abuse Claims*, Insight Books, New York, 1998

Ceci, S. & Bruck, M., *Jeopardy in the Courtroom: Scientific Analysis of Children's Testimony*, American Psychological Association, 1996

Crews, F., et al, *The Memory Wars: Freud's Legacy in Dispute*, Granta Books, London, 1997

Dineen, T., *Manufacturing Victims: What the Psychology Industry is Doing to People*, Constable & Co Ltd, 1999

Feltham, C., ed. *Controversies in Psychotherapy and Counselling*, Sage Publications Ltd, 1999

Loftus, M. & Ketchem, K., *The Myth of Repressed Memory: False Memories and Allegations of Sexual Abuse*, St. Martin's Press, 1994

McNally, R., *Remembering Trauma*, Belknap Harvard, 2003

Ofshe, R., Watters, E., *Making Monsters: False Memories, Psychotherapy and Sexual Hysteria*, Andre Deutsch, 1995

Pendergrast, M., *Victims of Memory: Incest Accusations and Shattered Lives*, HarperCollins, 1997

Pope, Jr., H.G., *Psychology Astray: Fallacies in Studies of "Repressed Memory" and Childhood Trauma*, Upton Books, 1997

Webster, R., *Why Freud Was Wrong: Sin, Science and Psychoanalysis*, HarperCollins, 1995

Yapko, M.D., *Suggestions of Abuse: True and False Memories of Childhood Sexual Trauma*, Simon & Schuster, 1994

Recommended Professional Articles

Brandon, S., Boakes, J., Glaser, D., and Green, R., 'Recovered memories of childhood sexual abuse: Implications for Clinical Practice', *The British Journal of Psychiatry* April 1998 Vol 172, 296-307

Kihlstrom, J.F., 'Trauma and memory revisited', Paper presented at the 6th Tsukuba International Conference on Memory: Memory and Emotion, March 2005. Note: An edited version appears in Uttl, B., Ohta, N., and Siegenthaler, A.L., (Eds) (2006). *Memory and Emotions: Interdisciplinary Perspectives*. New York: Blackwell.

McNally, R.J., 'Debunking myths about trauma and memory', *The Canadian Journal of Psychiatry*, 2005, 50, 817–822

McNally, R.J., 'Science and falsehood of traumatic amnesia' *Clinical Psychology: Science and Practice*, 2004. 11, 29-39

Pope, Jr, H.G., and Hudson, J.I., 'Can Memories of Childhood Sexual Abuse be Repressed?' *Psychological Medicine*, 1995, v.25, p. 121-126

Wright, D.B., Ost, J., and French, C., 'Recovered and false memories', *The Psychologist*, Vol 19 No. 6

Index

hospital/isation, 16, 24, 29, 33, 55, 58, 66, 67, 73, 78
hypnosis, 11, 71
incest, 69, 70
injunction, 34
inner self, 47
insurance money, 79
interview, 36, 51, 65, 66, 71, 76
investigative procedure, 67
malpractice, 32, 40, 77
mediator, 53
medical evidence, 36
Myalgic Encephalomyelitis (ME), 44
nervous breakdown, 69, 72
new age therapy, 62
obsessive compulsive disorder (OCD), 14
peer pressure, 12, 70
photograph, 36
police, 20, 26, 33-36, 51, 61, 64-66, 68-73
psychiatric unit, 29, 30, 71, 72
psychiatrist, 29, 53, 69, 70, 72, 74, 75, 77, 78, 82
psychologist, 20, 24, 34, 56, 66, 77, 79, 82
psychology of memory, 73
psychotherapy/ist, 15, 38, 42, 45, 48
psychotropic drugs, 30
Radio 4 (BBC), 16
reconciled, 37, 69, 74
recovered memory, 17, 18, 20, 40, 42, 67, 74, 75, 78, 82, 84, 85
regression therapy, 18, 41, 42, 62
repression, 18, 81, 82

retract/ion, 17, 49, 61, 69, 71, 74
returner, 34
Royal College of Psychiatrists (RCP), 18, 72
self-harming, 30, 33, 70, 84
self-help literature, 17, 18, 33, 62, 84, 85
separation, 29, 78
social services, 31, 32, 69, 71, 72
sodium amytal, 76
solicitor, 34, 36, 45, 56, 64-66, 75
sterilised, 77, 79
suggestion, 70, 71, 73, 76, 77, 81
suicide, 23, 24, 29, 31, 45, 54
The Courage to Heal, 18, 20, 27, 33, 34, 38, 45, 51, 53, 82, 84, 85
therapy/ist, 13-15, 17, 18, 23-25, 27-31, 38-45, 49, 52, 53, 55, 60, 62, 70, 77-82
trauma, 18, 82, 84
traumatic amnesia, 82
traumatic memories, 82
traumatic stress, 32, 43, 82
truth drug, 74
United Kingdom Council for Psychotherapy (UKCP), 18
Victims of Memory, 50
Weiskrantz, Professor Larry, 81-83
witness statements, 36
witness testimony, 81

Counselling or Quackery?

A personal view of the Therapy Industry and the Therapy Culture that underpins it.

William Burgoyne

www.pabd.com

Given the unregulated nature of the therapy and counselling industry inhabited by many practitioners with little or no training, it is inevitable that malpractice and abuse of the relationship between counsellor and client will occur. This can destroy the lives of those who have, innocently, placed their complete trust in their therapist to whom they have revealed their innermost thoughts and fears at a time when they are at their most vulnerable and suggestible. It can have a devastating effect on their parents, relatives and others who know the client and may be wrongly accused. This book attempts to provide an easily-read guide for parents and other secondary victims of therapy, and those who are contemplating therapy, are already receiving it or have experienced therapy but have doubts about their treatment.

Published by Publish and be Damned, 2006, ISBN 978 1905059515

Victims of Memory demonstrates how families are being torn apart by a
minority of mesmerizing, misguided analysts, using hypnosis, dreams and
persuasion to bend minds and unintentionally create false memories of
terrible events that never occurred.

Published by HarperCollins, 1996, ISBN 0 00 255684 7

Perhaps the most comprehensive study of the recovered memory movement... [Pendergrast's] book, richly documented and informed throughout
by a sense of history, is both wise and profound.

Richard Webster, *Why Freud Was Wrong*

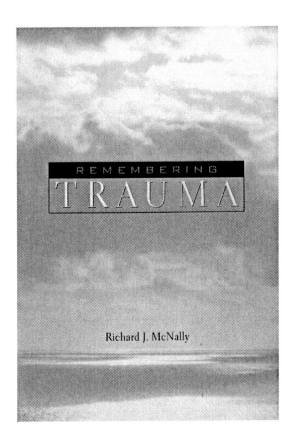

REMEMBERING
TRAUMA

Richard J. McNally

Are horrific experiences indelibly fixed in a victim's memory? Or does the
mind protect itself by banishing traumatic memories from consciousness?
How victims remember trauma is the most controversial issue in psychology today, spilling out of consulting rooms and laboratories to capture
headlines, rupture families, provoke legislative change, and influence
criminal trials and civil suits. This book, by a clinician who is also a laboratory researcher, is the first comprehensive, balanced analysis of the clinical
and scientific evidence bearing on this issue - and the first to provide
definitive answers to the urgent questions at the heart of the controversy.

Published by The Belknap Press, 2005, ISBN 978 0674018020

THE SCIENCE
OF FALSE MEMORY

C. J. Brainerd
V. F. Reyna

OXFORD PSYCHOLOGY SERIES

A decade or so of intensive research on false memory has revealed much that is not well understood outside the circles of scientists who specialise in such research. However, this research has produced findings that have major implications for a number of fields that are central to human welfare, such as medicine and the law. This book has been written to make those findings accessible to a much wider audience than research specialists, including child protective services workers, clinical psychologists, defense attorneys, teachers, general medical practitioners, journalists, judges, nurses, police investigators, prosecutors, and psychiatrists. For that reason, the book assumes little or no background knowledge in the techniques of memory research.

Published by Oxford University Press, 2005, ISBN 978 0195154054

THE SECRET OF
BRYN ESTYN

The making of a
modern witch hunt

RICHARD WEBSTER

A story of false accusations, judicial blindness, bad journalism and inno-cent lives destroyed. *The Secret of Bryn Estyn* tells the story of the greatest series of miscarriages of justice in recent British history - how innocent lives have been destroyed, the public deceived and millions of pounds wasted in a witch-hunt against innocent people.

Published by The Orwell Press, 2005, ISBN 978 0951592243

Printed in the United Kingdom
by Lightning Source UK Ltd.
119873UK00001B/13-147

9 780955 518409